LERNA

in the Argolid

Sauceboat, Lerna III

American School of Classical Studies at Athens

1997

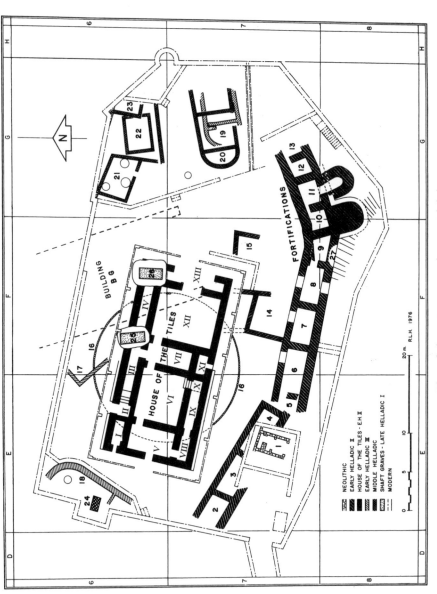

1. Plan of the main excavated area, with key

NEOLITHIC
EARLY HELLADIC II
HOUSE OF THE TILES - E.H.II
EARLY HELLADIC III
MIDDLE HELLADIC
SHAFT GRAVES - LATE HELLADIC I
MODERN

0   5   10   20 m.
RLH 1976

BUILDING
B G

HOUSE OF THE TILES

FORTIFICATIONS

N

2

Key to the Plan

1. House, Lerna II, early
2-13. Compartments in the fortification walls
14. Part of Room CA, Lerna III
15. Corner of Room DM, Lerna III
BG. Position of large building, Lerna III, early
16. Border of tumulus over the House of the Tiles, Lerna IV
17. Part of house over the tumulus, Lerna IV
18. Apsidal house, Lerna V
19. Apsidal house, Lerna IV–V
20. Apsidal house, Lerna V
21. Storeroom with pithoi, Lerna V
22, 23. Successive buildings, Lerna V
24. Grave, Lerna V, late
25. Shaft grave 1, Lerna VI
26. Shaft grave 2, Lerna VI
27. Position of kiln, Roman period

THE HOUSE OF THE TILES, Lerna III, late

I. Northwest storeroom
II. North entrance
III–IV. North corridor
V. Rear room
VI. Inner room
VII. Central room
VIII–X. South corridor
XI. South storeroom
XII. Main hall
XIII. Main entrance

Chronology

(APPROXIMATE DATES B.C., BY THE "HIGH CHRONOLOGY")

Lerna I = Early Neolithic = 6th–5th millennium (remains at lowest levels, not now visible).

Lerna II = Middle Neolithic = early 5th millennium (House 1, from earliest Middle Neolithic level). Traces of Late and Final Neolithic.

Traces of Early Helladic I, beginning of 3rd millennium.

Lerna III = Early Helladic II = middle of 3rd millennium (ca. 2750/2700–2300/2200; fortifications 2–13; House 14 [Room CA]; House 15 [Room DM]; Building BG; House of the Tiles [rooms I–XIII]).

Lerna IV = Early Helladic III = end of 3rd millennium (ca. 2300/2200–2050/2000; tumulus 16; Houses 17, 19 [Lerna IV–V]).

Lerna V = Middle Helladic = early 2nd millennium (2050/2000–1700/1675; Houses 18, 20–23).

Lerna VI = end of Middle Helladic and Late Helladic I = early 17th–early 16th century (shaft graves 1 and 2; 25, 26 on plan).

Remains of later Mycenaean times (Lerna VII = Late Helladic IIIA and IIIB), the Iron Age, and the Classical period were found but are not now visible (kiln 27 dates to the Roman period).

3

2. The site of Lerna, from the west

3. The main excavated area, from the northwest

The Site

The site of prehistoric Lerna is at the southeastern edge of the village of Myloi, about ten kilometers from Argos on the main highway to Tripolis (maps inside front and back covers). It appears as a broad, low mound, on which stands a conspicuous concrete structure that protects remains of a large ancient building, the so-called House of the Tiles (Fig. 2). Foothills of the Arcadian mountains are on the west; on the east are the railway lines and the shore of the Argolic Gulf. Lemon trees, now cut down, used to cover the northern part of the mound, the side closer to the village and the stream that issues from the Lernaean springs. Southward there is level ground. Visitors approach the site from the highway to the west, along a short path beside an orange grove.

Archaeological excavations were conducted at Lerna annually from 1952 to 1958 by Professor John L. Caskey and members of the American School of Classical Studies at Athens. The mound had been reduced over the centuries by erosion, and parts had been cut away by railway builders in 1891 and by military installations of World War II (plan, back cover). Large parts of the site were still undisturbed, however, and these were investigated selectively by the digging of pits and trenches and ultimately in more extended areas (Figs. 1, 3, back cover). Even so, only about one-seventh of the whole surface and one-twentieth of the volume of the mound were examined. When work was completed many of the excavated areas were refilled with earth.

In spite of these limitations, it became evident that the place had been occupied with few if any interruptions over a period of some 5,000 years, from the 6th to the 1st millennium B.C. Clearly, people chose to settle here because natural advantages were at hand: rich arable land; the sea for fishing and commerce; wood (from the mountains), stone, and clay for building; and, most important, an abundant source of fresh water.

At first a simple village occupied the site; later it grew in wealth and importance, but the community was never large by modern standards. At most there may have been 150 houses at any one time and a population of around 800.

Throughout the long period during which the site was occupied, with a few striking exceptions, the houses were small. Their walls were generally of packed clay or unfired bricks resting on rough stone foundations. The roofs, of which very little evidence survives, were probably of clay supported on wooden beams and light poles or reeds; some perhaps were thatched. When these buildings deteriorated or were destroyed by fire or earthquake, the plots where they had stood were leveled and new structures were erected, often incorporating parts of the older foundations and many of the fallen stones. Lying exposed to the elements, clay and crude brick soon dissolved and are now rarely discernible unless hardened accidentally in fires. Objects and refuse that had accumulated on floors or around the houses, and some quantities of debris from the destructions, were often left where they lay and so gradually raised the level of the ground. In fact, the whole mound of Lerna is made up of debris from successive layers of occupation.

4, 5. Neolithic figurine, front and back views

Tour of the Excavated Area

The plan in Figure 1 shows most of the structures that are now visible. Rooms and parts of buildings are marked by Arabic or Roman numerals. They are easily accessible within the fenced area. The House of the Tiles, inside a protective shelter that is closed to the public, may be viewed from outside.

For convenient reference, successive periods of human occupation at Lerna are designated by Roman numerals (Lerna I, II, etc.; see the chronological table, p. 3). In the following brief survey, examples of the architectural monuments are mentioned in sequence. Pots and other artifacts from the various habitation levels, on display in the Archaeological Museum in Argos, are described at the end of this account.

Neolithic
(LERNA I AND II)

Strata, or layers, representing the activities of the earliest inhabitants at Lerna (Lerna I = Early Neolithic) were examined in numerous deep trenches that were refilled when excavations ended. This is the period of the first settled farming communities. At Lerna, remains from this time include fragments of stone walls but no clearly defined buildings. The people used hand-built pottery that had been fired in open fires, and other tools of stone, bone, and baked clay. They planted grains; kept sheep, goats, pigs, and cattle; hunted wild boar, fox, hare, and birds; and gathered shellfish.

In the second Neolithic period (Lerna II = Middle Neolithic) the economy was similar and the community probably larger and more permanently settled. A well-built room, probably part of a house, can be seen in the deep pit near the entrance to the area (1 on the plan, Fig. 1). This was built early in Lerna II and was followed by a long succession of comparable buildings in this area. The pottery (Figs. 6, 7) was still hand built but more technically sophisticated and varied than earlier pottery (in Figure 7 note the dramatic "cloud" effect, produced by firing techniques). A number of pieces are distinguished by a mark in relief that surely carried some special meaning (Fig. 6:1, 2), many were

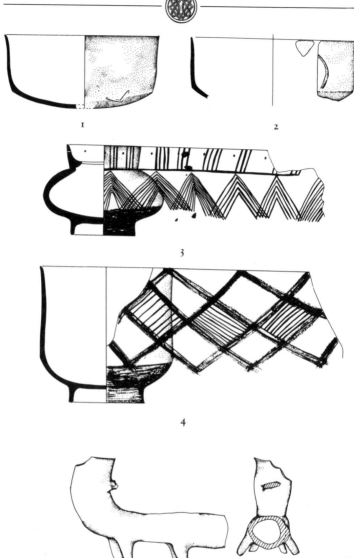

6. Neolithic pottery shapes
(1, 2: bowls with relief marks;
3, 4: patterned pottery;
5: animal vase)

7. Middle Neolithic jar with firing cloud

painted with geometric designs (Fig. 6:3, 4), and some are quite unusual (Fig. 6:5). An exceptionally fine, nearly complete terracotta figurine of a nude woman (Figs. 4, 5), standing with arms folded, came from one of the later phases of Lerna II.

Above the substantial accumulations from the Middle Neolithic period, only scattered traces of activities during the Late and Final Neolithic periods remain.

Ten graves were found, showing that children and adults were buried within the settlement, among the houses of the living, throughout the Neolithic period, from earliest to latest times.

The Bronze Age

The successive Bronze Age periods at Lerna are known in archaeological terms as the Early, Middle, and Late Helladic periods and cover the time span from approximately 3000 to 1100 B.C.

Early Helladic II
(LERNA III)

The Early Helladic settlements followed the Neolithic one and spanned much of the third millennium B.C. This period is currently divided into three stages (I, II, III). There seems to have been some occupation of the site in Early Helladic I times, since a few scattered potsherds of that period have been found in later levels, but no remains of habitation have yet been discovered. At some time not long after the beginning of the Early Helladic II period, the settlers began a long process of leveling and filling the uneven surface of the mound and constructing some substantial buildings and heavy walls to enclose or fortify the settlement. Excavation uncovered many successive building levels of Early Helladic II. The majority of the remains visible today belong to the latter part of that period, of which the culminating architectural achievement was the House of the Tiles (described below).

8. Room CA, Early Helladic II pottery as found in place

9. Pithos from Room DM, Early Helladic II

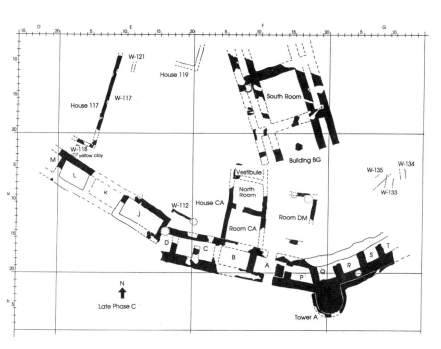

10. Lerna III, Early Helladic II, late phase C,
preceding the House of the Tiles, main area

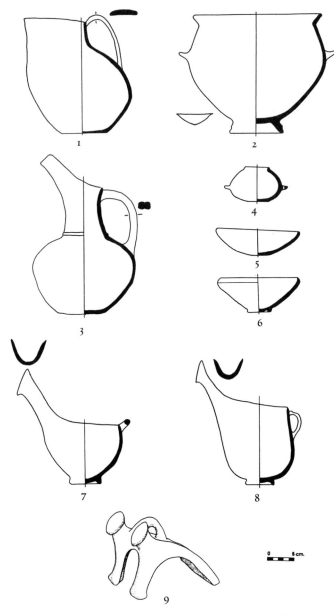

11. Lerna III, Early Helladic II pottery shapes (1: askos; 2: collared bowl; 3: jug; 4: pyxis; 5, 6: saucers; 7, 8: sauceboats; 9: cooking stand)

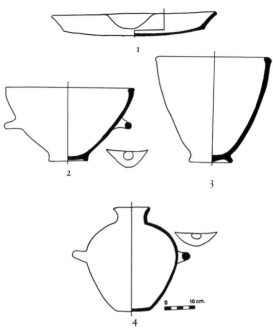

12. Lerna III, Early Helladic II pottery shapes
(1: baking pan; 2: basin; 3: bowl; 4: jar)

To the left of the entrance gate, a line of three rooms, 2–4, can be seen above the Neolithic house; then a similar row of rooms, 5–13, continuing eastward. These made up parts of an enclosure or fortification system that probably surrounded the whole site. The rooms or compartments within it, formed by crosswalls between the continuous inner and outer walls, served as living and storage areas. If covered by a flat roof, these perhaps had outer parapets that may have served for defense.

The oldest parts of the circuit wall, which was altered and rebuilt several times, are toward the east, rooms 9–13 in Figure 1 (Q–T, Fig. 10). From 11 there was access to a U-shaped tower. Past this, on the outside, a stepped, stone roadway came up from the southeast, probably from the shore, to a gateway that preceded the one visible at room 8 (A, Fig. 10). After a time this tower was demolished and was replaced by another one, heavier and solid, that stood south of room 10 and covered parts of the old steps. Fires damaged the walls at various times, hardening some of the crude brick used above the stone foundations. It is now protected by copings of modern tiles.

Many buildings stood within the circuit wall. Just north of room 7 are walls of a house, 14 (Room CA, Fig. 10), that had at least two rooms, and nearby is a corner of another, 15 (Room DM). A number of others were found but have been reburied to protect their crumbling remains. Several of these buildings had been destroyed by fires, their earthen floors blackened and strewn with ashes and household implements (Room CA, Fig. 8).

The pottery of this period, still handmade, is plain but carefully designed (Figs. 11, 12). The finest pieces are smooth, often polished, and well fired. Painted decoration was rare. Asymmetrical shapes such as the so-called sauceboat (title page and Fig. 11:7, 8), the askos (a type of pitcher, Fig. 11:1), and coarse cooking stands (Fig. 11:9) are characteristic. Pithoi, man-sized storage jars, were common (Fig. 9). Examples of these and other Early Helladic II shapes may be seen at the museum.

Parts of a monumental building, Building **BG** (Fig. 10), were discovered in soundings that, owing to the condition of the masonry and other considerations, had to be refilled. Its position, chiefly in square F 6, is indicated by broken lines on the plan in Figure 1; the northern end of Building BG was not excavated. The main entrance, within an open porch, was at the southern end of the building, facing the circuit walls. This large structure was surely a forerunner and prototype of the later House of the Tiles.

The House of the Tiles
(LERNA III)

In one of the first small trenches dug in 1952 the corner of a very large building was uncovered. In subsequent years more of it was revealed until, in 1955, the whole plan was exposed. Rectangular clay tiles that had covered its roof lay everywhere in the fallen debris, and the building came to be known as the House of the Tiles, a name that has endured. (Many fragments of these tiles now fill in gaps in the walls caused by damage in ancient times.)

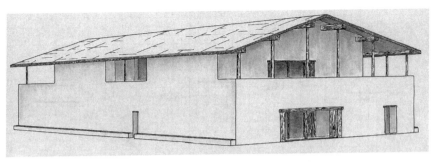

13. Reconstruction of the House of the Tiles,
view from the southeast

The House of the Tiles belongs to the latest phase of Lerna III, a time when Building BG, Rooms CA and DM, and perhaps other rooms had been demolished and when even the circuit walls were out of repair. The building itself was unfinished on the day it was destroyed by the fire that marks the end of the Early Helladic II period at the site.

The House of the Tiles (Fig. 13 and front cover) is oriented roughly east–west and is about 25 meters long and 12 meters wide. The lower parts of the walls, some 90 centimeters thick, are fairly well preserved: firm stone foundations support the upper wall courses, built of crude mud bricks baked hard in the blaze. Clay benches stood against the outer faces of the north and south walls. Visitors can readily see the chief features of the house by walking around the enclosure.

A main hall, XII on the plan in Figure 1, was entered through a wide doorway and vestibule, room XIII. From here doorways gave passage to rooms on the central axis, V–VII, and the rear door at the west. From room VII one could enter a long corridor, III–IV, on the north side (the big graves, 25 and 26 in Figure 1, were dug down through the walls at a much later date). Room V gave access to the shorter southern corridor, VIII–X. Two very small rooms, I, at the northwest corner, and XI, at the middle of the south side, could be entered only from outside. The building clearly had a second story: a doorway in the north wall led to a staircase rising in the north corridor, III–IV; and another flight of stairs, giving access from indoors, rose from the southeast corner of room VI, leading first southward and then turning westward within the south corridor, VIII–X. If the heavy walls supported similar walls on the second story, as seems likely, then the major room of the house may have been that above the large ground-floor room, XII, and was therefore approached by the north stairway. Balconies may have encircled parts of the house at the second-story level above the corridors, providing light to the inner rooms. In fact, room VII may have been a kind of "light well," open to the rafters. It would appear that the front rooms, XIII and XII, and those above them formed a "public" unit, distinct from the more "private" back rooms, VI and V, and the second-story floor spaces above them, which were served by the narrow back door and the inner stairway.

The well-fired terracotta roof tiles, about one centimeter thick, were rectangular, flat, and unpierced. They were laid overlapping like shingles on a bedding of clay that was supported by large wooden beams and a lattice of smaller timbers. The roof was undoubtedly gently pitched, probably gabled like that of the modern shelter. Fragments of the tiles, which were found by the thousands, may be seen where they fell in room XII; fragments of many others were used by the archaeologists to fill gaps in the damaged walls. Besides the broken tiles, slabs of schist lay in the debris, chiefly along the sides of the building. Small holes had been drilled in many of these, probably in order to peg them to the rafters. They may have been set as eaves, projecting beyond the walls of the house in order to shed rainwater.

In spite of the ruined state of the House of the Tiles, some architectural refinements can be observed. Floors were composed of thick layers of fine yellow clay. Walls were coated with smooth lime plaster or were about to be plastered. At the time of the fire most had only been prepared by scoring, but in room XII and the northwest entrance, II, and in the western end of the north staircase, the final surface of plaster had been applied. A few horizontal and vertical lines were incised on the surfaces of the walls in the main room, producing zones and panels, but no traces of wall paintings have been detected. Jambs of the doorway to room XII, of the east doorway into room VII, and of the northwest entrance, II, were sheathed with wood (the partial replacements are modern).

The usual types of Early Helladic II pottery (see p. 14 and Fig. 11) were present but not plentiful, nor were there many tools or household implements. Only one group of objects is notable: a large collection of

14, 15, 16. Designs of seal impressions (*CMS* V.1, nos. 57, 109, 111; reproduced with the permission of the Corpus der minoischen und mykenischen Siegel, all rights reserved)

broken clay sealings that were used to secure wooden chests and storage jars. These sealings had been hardened by the fire and thus preserved impressions of over 60 elaborately and delicately carved seals used to stamp them after they were affixed to chests and jars (Figs. 14, 15, 16). Almost all the sealings were found in the small outer room, XI.

The House of the Tiles was erected as a successor to Building BG, apparently at a time when parts of the settlement were to be rebuilt. Construction had reached the roof, and tiles were in place. As noted, ground-floor rooms were still being finished at the time of the fire; the state of the upper floor cannot be known. For some reason sealed containers of valuable goods were already being stored in the small room XI. Then came the final conflagration, fed by structural timbers and perhaps by temporary scaffoldings and other flammable substances.

We do not know what caused the fire, although some speculation is possible. Certain other sites in Greece were destroyed around this same time. Some of these sites in southern Greece had buildings like the House of the Tiles, which have come to be known as "corridor houses," notably Kolonna on the island of Aigina, where part of a similar house may be seen, and Akovitika near Kalamata. The resources that allowed the leveling and building programs culminating in these large structures certainly indicate a well-organized society possessed of a certain amount of power, which may well have encouraged rivalry and aggression. The dismantled circuit walls at Lerna would have provided no defense. There are indications, too, that new peoples, perhaps from Asia Minor, were moving into parts of Greece. However the fire may be explained, it was catastrophic and marked the end of an era.

Early Helladic III
(LERNA IV)

The Tumulus

After the great destruction there was a distinct change of inhabitants and way of life at Lerna: there were no more fortifications or monumental buildings, and houses, pots, and tools were quite different. This is the Early Helladic III period in archaeological terms.

Most remains of this period had to be removed during the course of excavation. Strangest and most notable among those now visible are curving rows of rounded stones (Fig. 1:16, 20), best seen just to the north and south of the House of the Tiles. Other stones of the same series were found within the area of that building, appreciably above the level of the ground floor. These stones mark the circumference of a circle about nineteen meters in diameter, bordering a low convex mound, or tumulus, of fallen debris from the House of the Tiles; the surface of the mound was strewn with small stones and pebbles.

Why this carefully wrought monument? The shape suggests a funerary tumulus, but no human burials were found in it, only the ruins of the House of the Tiles, over which it was centered with remarkable accuracy (Fig. 17). That the place was regarded for some time with awe or veneration is indicated by the fact that houses of Lerna IV were built around the tumulus but did not encroach upon the ground within. Only after some time had passed did people begin to build over it (see, for example, the walls of House 17 in squares E–F 6, Fig 1).

The Settlement of Lerna IV

Houses of the fourth settlement were usually long and freestanding, with the doorway situated at one end within an open porch, the other end closed by an apse. A crosswall might divide the semicircular space at the back of the house from the main rectangular room, in which there was often a round hearth. The apsidal form was new at this site, though much older elsewhere (occurring, for example, many centuries earlier in the most ancient settlement at the citadel of Troy). Many houses of this kind were found at Lerna, with small houses often satellite to large ones, no doubt reflecting familial or social groupings within

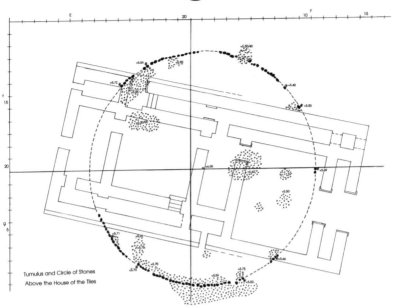

Tumulus and Circle of Stones
Above the House of the Tiles

17. Circle of stones over the House of the Tiles

the community. Remains of one house (19), built in a late phase of Lerna IV, lie beneath a similar house of Lerna V (20), toward the east in square G 7. Between House 20 and the House of the Tiles some further remnants of house walls can be seen.

Pottery and other objects of the Early Helladic III period show new forms and techniques. Vessels are now sometimes thrown on the wheel rather than built by hand; symmetrical shapes are favored; and the vessels more frequently have painted decoration (Figs. 18, 19, 21). A special find from a rubbish pit associated with one of the earliest apsidal houses of Lerna IV is a fragmentary two-handled bell-shaped cup made of banded marble, with a small removable disk drilled out of the center of its bottom. It is known as the Chieftain Cup (Fig. 20). With this disk removed, the cup would function as a rhyton, a vessel used for drinking or perhaps to make libations.

The transition to the fifth settlement at Lerna (Lerna V) marks the beginning of the Middle Helladic period and is less sharply marked than were earlier transitions. Some features of the Lerna IV culture were carried over, but new ones appeared as well.

18. Goblet of Lerna IV

19. Three-spouted jar, Lerna IV

20. Stone Chieftain Cup, Lerna IV

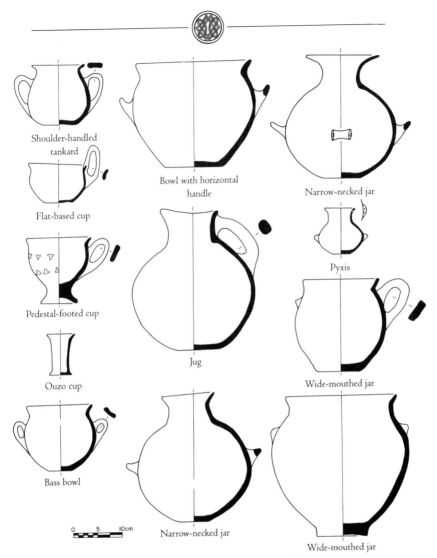

Shoulder-handled tankard

Flat-based cup

Pedestal-footed cup

Ouzo cup

Bass bowl

Bowl with horizontal handle

Jug

Narrow-necked jar

Narrow-necked jar

Pyxis

Wide-mouthed jar

Wide-mouthed jar

0   5   10cm

21. Lerna IV, Early Helladic III pottery shapes

21

Middle Helladic
(LERNA V)

The inhabitants of Lerna continued to thrive throughout the Middle Bronze Age, changing but little in the manner in which they lived and worked. As the years went by, however, the village became increasingly prosperous, certainly in part because of exploitation of the rich farmland of the Argive plain and the growing importance of this coastal site as a market for traders sailing into the Bay of Argos. With these traders came new types of artifacts and pottery from other areas of the Aegean—from the islands of Kythera, Crete, the Cyclades, and Aigina (Figs. 22–25). Imports from the island of Aigina were especially plentiful throughout the Middle and early Late Helladic periods and included various types of pottery and millstones of andesite, the volcanic stone of the island. The Aeginetans produced a complete range of vases for use in the household: fine tablewares and storage jars and cooking pots for the kitchen. The large quantities of Aeginetan imports found at Lerna and many other sites on the Mainland indicate that Aigina had a flourishing industry producing ceramics for export.

In addition to island imports, pots manufactured locally and in other areas of the the Mainland, both the southern Peloponnesos and Central Greece, were found in the households and burials of Lerna V. Among these finds are Lerna IV wares that continued to be produced and new wares that have become hallmarks of the Middle Helladic period in Greece: handmade Matt Painted and wheel-thrown Gray Minyan. Manufacture by hand, perhaps with the aid of a turntable, was the chosen method of Mainland potters; throwing on a wheel,

22. Dark-burnished kantharos, Peloponnesian manufacture

23. Polychrome bridge-spouted jar (Kamares Ware), Minoan import

24. Matt Painted bird jug, Cycladic import

25. Matt Painted barrel jar, Aeginetan import

26. Roofing clay from room 21

commonly practiced on Crete and Kythera, appears to have been used on the Mainland only by potters in Central Greece until the Late Helladic period.

The houses of Lerna V were built in the same way as those of Lerna IV and followed the same settlement plan. Some of the houses were large, like House 18, one of the earliest buildings of the period. Another apsidal house, removed during excavation of deeper layers to the east of the House of the Tiles, was part of a complex that included an enclosed courtyard with a cooking area and a storehouse, room 21, that contained large pithoi. The house and its outbuildings were destroyed by fire. As a result, some roofing clay (Fig. 26) and wall bricks were baked and preserved, as were impressions of a wooden doorjamb in room 21 (replaced in the modern reconstruction).

Two superimposed apsidal houses, Houses 19 and 20, and the rooms to the north, room 22 and the later room 23, provide evidence for the dense sequence of building and rebuilding encountered in excavation of levels of the latest Early Helladic period (House 19) and the long Middle Helladic period, from the 21st to the early 17th century B.C.

In Lerna V the dead were buried within the settlement. By the middle phases of the period, and continuing into Lerna VI, they were buried in stone-built cists like grave 24, which dates to the end of Lerna V. Many of these graves appear to have been placed together to form a cemetery within the settlement.

The End of Middle Helladic and the Beginning of the Late Helladic Period
(LERNA VI)

Remains of Lerna VI, the transitional phase between the late Middle Helladic period and the early Late Helladic period, were found in trenches northeast of the present archaeological site. (Remains of this period are scanty because of the destruction wrought by erosion and by ancient and modern activity on the mound.) At this time (early 17th to early 16th century B.C.) larger houses with multiple rooms were constructed, at least one of them equipped with a built drain. The improvement in architectural practices and living conditions, along with the increased amount of disposable wealth apparent in grave offerings, is an indication of the changing economic status of the inhabitants of Lerna. This is the period made famous by the stupendous display of wealth in the Shaft Graves at Mycenae.

Two shaft graves like those at Mycenae were discovered at Lerna. Outlines of the shafts of these graves, shaft graves 25 and 26 (in Fig. 1), were recognized near the present surface of the mound. This means that when the graves were dug the ground level was at least as high as it is now, quite possibly higher still. The shafts had cut through the layers of Lerna V and IV and into Lerna III levels, destroying house walls of each period. The fillings held thousands of potsherds from vessels in styles characteristic of Lerna VI. At the bottom were the stone-lined graves, each with a flooring of white pebbles. Two fine, small cups lay on the floor in 26 (Fig. 27), but there were none in 25. There were no

27. Cups from shaft grave 26

skeletons in either grave and, in striking contrast to the riches of the royal graves of Mycenae, no precious objects. Quite obviously, the Lerna graves had been emptied in ancient times, either by grave robbers or possibly by the people of a later generation, who were perhaps moving to another site and wanted to take with them the bones of their heroic ancestors.

Late Helladic
(LERNA VII)

Excavation on the eastern side of the site, toward the railway line and northeast of the area that is now exposed, revealed walls of houses and other remains of habitation dating to the 14th and 13th centuries (Late Helladic IIIA and IIIB), the period called Lerna VII (a bowl typical of the Late Helladic III period can be seen in Figure 28). There was probably a flourishing town at Lerna at this time, satellite perhaps to the larger Mycenaean center of Argos, but much of it has been lost through

28. Bowl, Late Helladic III

erosion. A few graves and other scattered evidence from other parts of the mound indicate the extent of the Late Helladic III settlement and some restricted occupation during the earlier Late Helladic II period.

Post-Mycenaean

Well shafts, a few graves, and a scattering of recognizable objects provide evidence that the site was occupied to some extent in the Early Iron Age and in Classical Greek and Roman Imperial times. The visible remnants are scanty. What looks like a niche in the Early Helladic circuit wall, 27 in square F 8, shows where a round lime kiln was built against the hillside in the Roman period. A cemetery of the Geometric period (9th–8th centuries B.C.) was spread over the lower slopes of Mount Pontinos, some 400 meters west of the site.

The Lerna Collection in the
Archaeological Museum at Argos

Objects found at Lerna are on display in a corridor and gallery on the ground floor in the western part of the museum. From the front entrance one goes to the right through a large gallery containing exhibits from Argos. A passage and stairway lead to a fine old mansion, the Kallergeion, which has been remodeled as part of the museum. In the corridor leading to the main exhibition room are Geometric pithoi standing on the floor and Middle Helladic (Lerna V) barrel jars (in the Aeginetan Matt Painted style) in niches.

In the main exhibition room pots and other objects are generally arranged in chronological sequence, proceeding clockwise. (The room has three windows on the west and two on the north.)

1. Wall case to the left as one enters: Neolithic wares, the earliest, Lerna I, on the top shelf, those of Lerna II below.

2. Small case on a pedestal: terracotta statuette of a woman (Figs. 4, 5), the head and lower right leg missing (preserved height 18.20 cm.). Middle Neolithic (Lerna II).

3. Under the central left-hand window: Middle Helladic (Lerna V) Matt Painted Aeginetan storage jar.

4. Wall case: wares chiefly of the earlier phases of Early Helladic II (Lerna III), the walled settlement.

5. Near the center of the room: large, round ceremonial hearth, the rim decorated with an impressed zigzag pattern. It was found in Building BG (Early Helladic II); the central depression contained ashes.

6. In the far left-hand corner: large pithos from Room DM (15, Fig. 1), Early Helladic II (Lerna III); see Figure 9.

7. Case against the wall opposite the entrance: objects of the Early Helladic II period. Note, at the left, a lentoid flask with painted decoration; at the right, a roof tile and clay sealings from the House of the Tiles.

8. Near the window, far right: three-spouted ceremonial drinking vessel of Early Helladic III (Lerna IV); see Figure 19.

9. At the right-hand wall: wall case with pottery of the Early Helladic III (Lerna IV) period.

10. Freestanding case nearest the last: pottery of the Early Helladic III period. Note the red-brown jar with winglike projections, probably imported from Troy.

11. At the wall: Bichrome Matt Painted jar, from the transitional phase between the Early Helladic III (Lerna IV) and the Middle Helladic (Lerna V) periods.

12. Freestanding case: Middle Helladic pottery of Lerna V. Along with local wares, note the vessels imported from other areas of Greece: from the Cyclades (Melos), a duck vase and bird jug; from Crete, Middle Minoan Kamares ware; from Aigina, Matt Painted and Red Slipped and Burnished wares; from the southern Peloponnesos and Kythera, Lustrous Decorated (Minoanizing) and Dark Burnished wares (flasks with incised decoration); from Central Greece, true wheel-thrown Gray Minyan ware.

13, 14. At the wall: Middle Helladic (Lerna V) Matt Painted storage jar (13) and Coarse storage jar with bung hole (14).

15. Wall case to the left as one faces the entrance: pottery of the transitional period from the end of the Middle Helladic to the early

Late Helladic period (Lerna VI) on the two upper shelves; note the imported pottery found in Lerna V, especially Lustrous Decorated (Minoanizing) and Aeginetan wares (Matt Painted, Red Slipped and Burnished, and Coarse cooking pots). On the third shelf, wares of the Late Helladic III period, the time during which the citadels at nearby Argos, Mycenae, Tiryns, and Midea flourished. Geometric and Classical wares are below.

16. Beside the doorway: Lerna V Aeginetan Matt Painted barrel jar, which was used as a container for the burial of a four-year-old child.

Publications

FINAL PUBLICATIONS

Volumes in the series of definitive reports on Lerna are published by the American School of Classical Studies at Athens. The following have appeared:

Lerna: A Preclassical Site in the Argolid

   I = N.-G. Gejvall, *The Fauna*, Princeton 1969

   II = J. L. Angel, *The People*, Princeton 1971

   III = J. B. Rutter, *The Pottery of Lerna IV*, Princeton 1995

   IV = M. H. Wiencke, *The Stratification, Architecture, and Pottery of Lerna III*, Princeton, in press

DISSERTATIONS

E. C. Banks, *The Early and Middle Helladic Small Objects from Lerna* (University of Cincinnati 1967; University Microfilms International 67-15948)

E. T. Blackburn, *Middle Helladic Graves and Burial Customs with Special Reference to Lerna in the Argolid* (University of Cincinnati 1970; University Microfilms International 71-01536)

W. Donovan, *A Study of Early Helladic Pottery with Painted Decoration* (University of Cincinnati 1961; University Microfilms International 61-5219)

C. W. Zerner, *The Beginning of the Middle Helladic Period at Lerna* (University of Cincinnati 1978; University Microfilms International 79-04772)

PRELIMINARY EXCAVATION REPORTS

See J. L. Caskey's preliminary reports on the Lerna excavations in *Hesperia*, vols. 23–28, 1954–1959.

FURTHER PUBLICATIONS ON LERNA

E. C. Banks, "Neolithic *Tangas* from Lerna," *Hesperia* 47, 1978, pp. 324–339

J. L. Caskey, "The Early Helladic Period in the Argolid," *Hesperia* 29, 1960, pp. 285–303

M. C. Caskey, "Thoughts on Early Bronze Age Hearths," in *Celebration of Death and Divinity in the Bronze Age Argolid*, R. Hägg and G. C. Nordquist, eds., Stockholm 1990, pp. 13–21

J. K. Kozlowski, M. Kaczanowska, and M. Pawlikowski, "Chipped-Stone Industries from Neolithic Levels at Lerna," *Hesperia* 65, 1996, pp. 295–372

C. Runnels, "The Bronze Age Flaked-Stone Industries from Lerna: A Preliminary Report," *Hesperia* 54, 1985, pp. 357–391

J. B. Rutter, *Ceramic Change in the Aegean Early Bronze Age* (UCLA, Institute of Archaeology, Occasional Paper 5), Los Angeles 1979

J. B. Rutter, "Fine Gray-Burnished Pottery of the Early Helladic III Period: The Ancestry of Gray Minyan," *Hesperia* 52, 1983, pp. 327–355

K. D. Vitelli, "Neolithic Potter's Marks from Lerna and the Franchthi Cave," *Journal of the Walters Art Gallery* 36, 1977, pp. 17–30

M. H. Wiencke, "Lerna," in *Corpus der minoischen und mykenischen Siegel*, V.1, *Kleinere Griechische Sammlungen*, I. Pini, ed., Berlin 1975, pp. 28–32, 36–114

M. H. Wiencke, "Change in Early Helladic II," *American Journal of Archaeology* 93, 1989, pp. 495–509

C. W. Zerner, "Middle Helladic and Late Helladic I Pottery from Lerna," *Hydra* 2, 1986, pp. 58–73

C. W. Zerner, "Middle Helladic and Late Helladic I Pottery from Lerna: Part II: Shapes," *Hydra* 4, 1988, pp. 1–10

FOR FURTHER READING

G. Cadogan, ed., *The End of the Early Bronze Age in the Aegean*, Leiden 1986

J.-P. Demoule and C. Perlès, "The Greek Neolithic: A New Review," *Journal of World Prehistory* 7, 1993, pp. 355–416

J. Forsén, *The Twilight of the Early Helladics: A Study of the Disturbances in East-Central and Southern Greece towards the End of the Early Bronze Age*, Jonsered 1992

R. Hägg and D. Konsola, eds., *Early Helladic Architecture and Urbanization* (*Studies in Mediterranean Archaeology* 76), Göteborg 1986

S. Manning, *The Absolute Chronology of the Aegean Early Bronze Age: The Evidence of Archaeology, Cultural Interrelations, and Radiocarbon*, Sheffield 1993

G. A. Papathanassopoulos, ed., *Neolithic Culture in Greece* (N. P. Goulandris Museum/Museum of Cycladic Art), Athens 1996

J. B. Rutter, "Review of Aegean Prehistory II: The Prepalatial Bronze Age of the Southern and Central Greek Mainland," *American Journal of Archaeology* 97, 1993, pp. 745–797

J. W. Shaw, "The Early Helladic II Corridor House: Development and Form," *American Journal of Archaeology* 91, 1987, pp. 59–79

Illustrations

Front cover: reconstruction of the House of the Tiles
Inside front cover: Argolic Gulf and Argive Plain
Frontispiece: sauceboat, Lerna III
1. Plan of the main excavated area, with key
2. The site of Lerna, from the west
3. The main excavated area, from the northwest
4, 5. Neolithic figurine, front and back views
6. Neolithic pottery shapes (1, 2: bowls with relief marks;
3, 4: patterned pottery; 5: animal vase)
7. Middle Neolithic jar with firing cloud
8. Room CA, Early Helladic II pottery as found in place
9. Pithos from Room DM, Early Helladic II
10. Lerna III, Early Helladic II, late phase C,
preceding the House of the Tiles, main area
11. Lerna III, Early Helladic II pottery shapes (1: askos; 2: collared bowl;
3: jug; 4: pyxis; 5, 6: saucers; 7, 8: sauceboats; 9: cooking stand)
12. Lerna III, Early Helladic II pottery shapes
(1: baking pan; 2: basin; 3: bowl; 4: jar)
13. Reconstruction of the House of the Tiles, view from the southeast
14, 15, 16. Designs of seal impressions (*CMS* V.1, nos. 57, 109, 111)
17. Circle of stones over the House of the Tiles
18. Goblet of Lerna IV
19. Three-spouted jar, Lerna IV
20. Stone Chieftain Cup, Lerna IV
21. Lerna IV, Early Helladic III pottery shapes
22. Dark-burnished kantharos, Peloponnesian manufacture
23. Polychrome bridge-spouted jar (Kamares Ware), Minoan import
24. Matt Painted bird jug, Cycladic import
25. Matt Painted barrel jar, Aeginetan import
26. Roofing clay from room 21
27. Cups from shaft grave 26
28. Bowl, Late Helladic III
Inside back cover: map of the Argive Plain in prehistoric times,
with palaeo-coastline and the former Lake Lerna
Back cover: contour plan of site

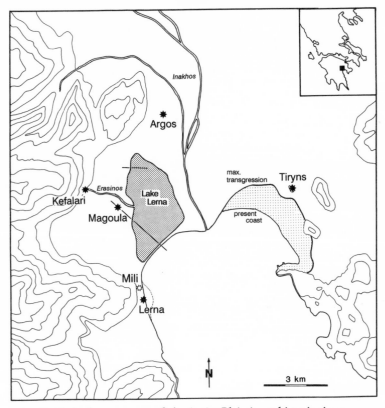

Inside back cover: map of the Argive Plain in prehistoric times,
with palaeo-coastline and the former Lake Lerna, after Zangger 1991
(reproduced with the permission of the *Journal of Field Archaeology* and
Trustees of Boston University, all rights reserved)

Back cover: contour plan of site

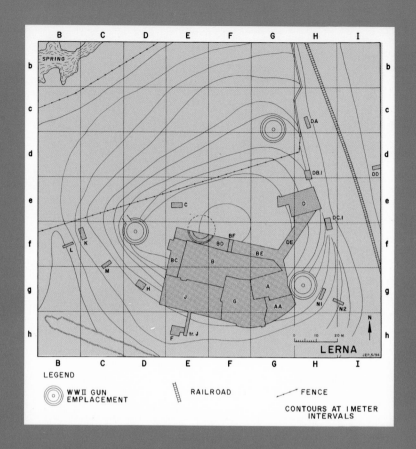

LERNA

JEP.5/94

LEGEND

◎ WW II GUN
    EMPLACEMENT

▦ RAILROAD

╱ FENCE

CONTOURS AT 1 METER
INTERVALS

ISBN 087661-680-5